25 YEAR Celebration of MANNHEIM STEAMROLLER

DOTS AND LINES, INK

9130 MORMON BRIDGE ROAD OMAHA, NEBRASKA 68152 402.457.4341

www.amgram.com

EXCLUSIVELY DISTRIBUTED BY

HAL•LEONARD® CORPORATION

7777 W. BLUEMOUND RD. P.O. BOX 13819 MILWAUKEE, WI 53213

Visit Hal Leonard Online at
www.halleonard.com

THE STEAMROLLER

from FRESH AIRE 8

By CHIP DAVIS

Brightly, with a groove (♩ = 134)

MORNING
from FRESH AIRE III

By CHIP DAVIS

BAROQUE-A-NOVA
from CLASSICAL GAS

Music by MASON WILLIAMS
Arranged by CHIP DAVIS

Brightly ($\quad$ = 152)

CHRISTMAS LULLABY
from CHRISTMAS IN THE AIRE

By CHIP DAVIS

Simply

mp

With pedal

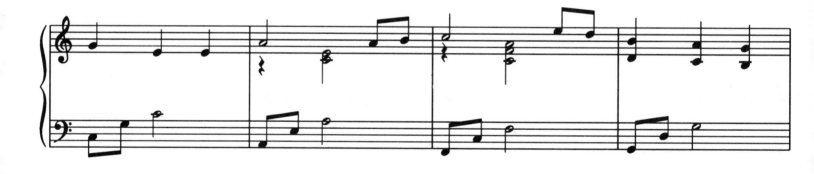

FOUR ROWS OF JACKS
from FRESH AIRE IV

By CHIP DAVIS

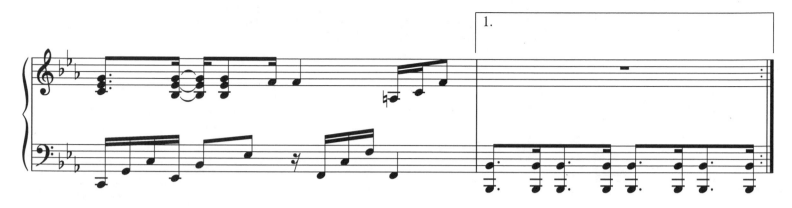

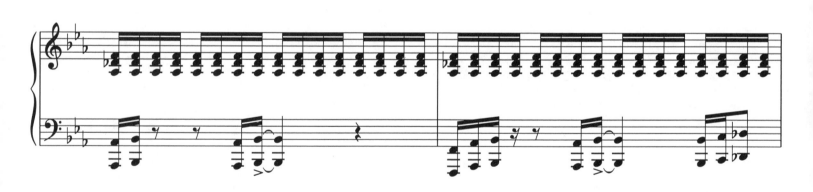

CHOCOLATE COFFEE
from SUNDAY MORNING COFFEE II

By CHIP DAVIS

Moderately (♩ = 104)

Drum break

Drums

A WINTER'S DAY
from IMPRESSIONS

By CHIP DAVIS

Rather freely

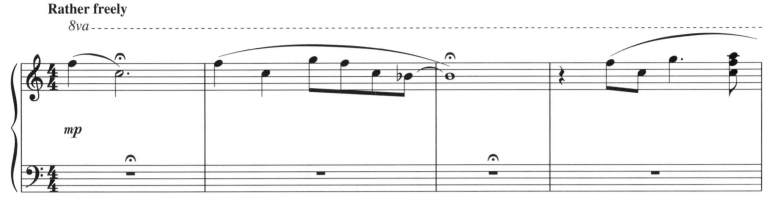

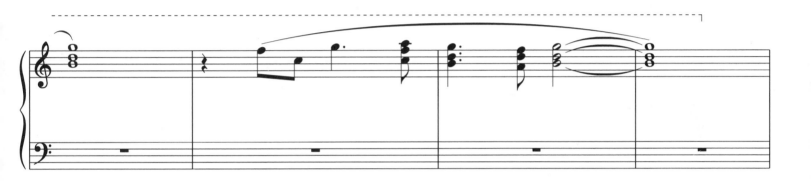

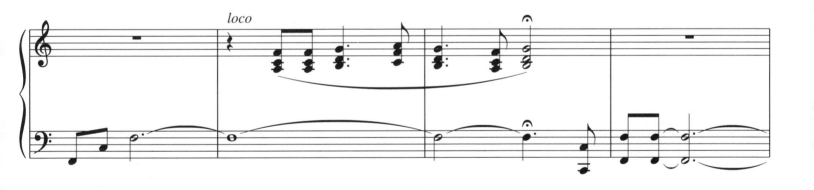

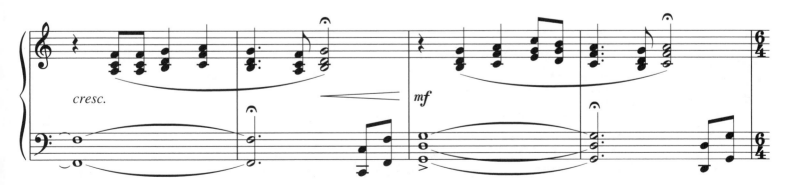

Evenly and flowing

mp

MORNING BLEND
from SUNDAY MORNING COFFEE

By CHIP DAVIS

Steadily (♩=94)

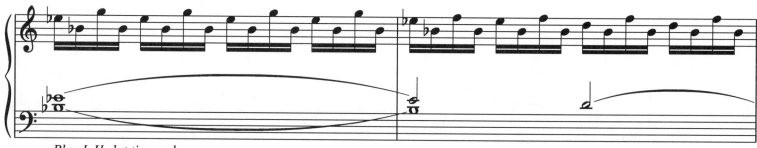

Play L.H. 1st time only

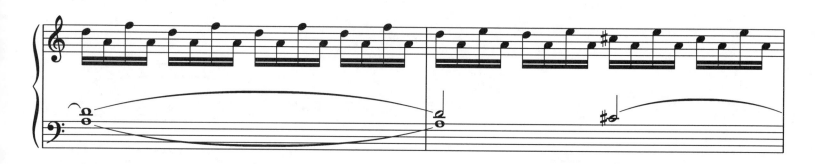

Play both times

To Coda ⊕

D.C. al Coda

Drums

CODA *Fade or play to ending*

INTERLUDE I
from INTERLUDES

By CHIP DAVIS

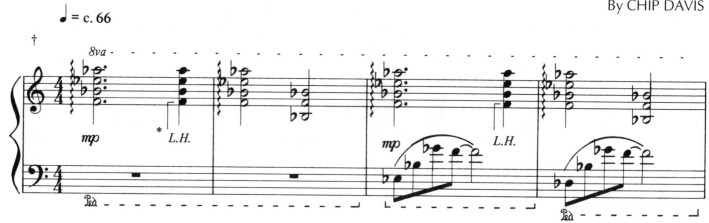

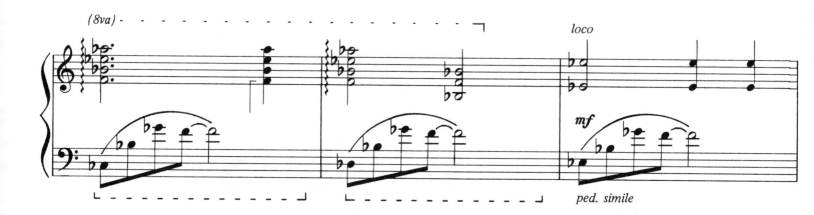

† Interlude 1 uses a 4-note ostinato pattern in the right hand.
* Take bottom note of chord in left hand, as indicated.

REGGAE MAÑANA MON
from PARTY

By CHIP DAVIS

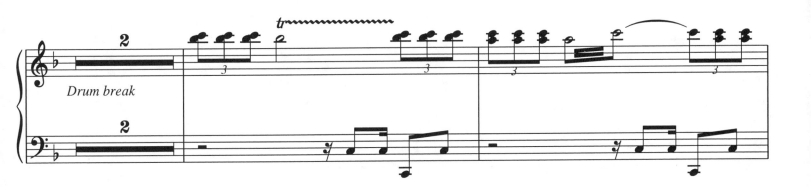

simile

Drum break

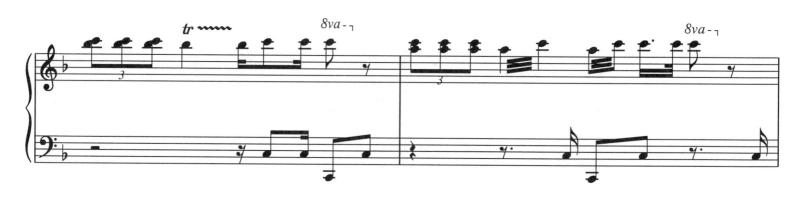

PRELUDE
from FRESH AIRE I

By CHIP DAVIS

SEGUE TO **Chocolate Fudge**

* Ed. note: Start with a full pedal and release slowly, as indicated by dotted line.

CHOCOLATE FUDGE

from FRESH AIRE I

By CHIP DAVIS

← ♪ = ♪ →

Slower (swing feel)

rit.

8va bassa 2nd time -

(8va bassa 2nd time) - - - - - - - - - - - - - - - - ⌐

(loco)

SLO DANCIN' IN THE LIVING ROOM

from ROMANCE II

By CHIP DAVIS

Slow and smoothly (♩ = 60)

PINES OF ROME
I. The Pines of the Villa Borghese
from YELLOWSTONE: THE MUSIC OF NATURE

By OTTORINO RESPIGHI

cresc. al fine

TWILIGHT AT RHODES

from FRESH AIRE VI

By CHIP DAVIS

ZIP-A-DEE-DOO-DAH
from MANNHEIM STEAMROLLER MEETS THE MOUSE

Words by RAY GILBERT
Music by ALLIE WRUBEL
Arranged by CHIP DAVIS

Moderately ($\quad$ = 126)

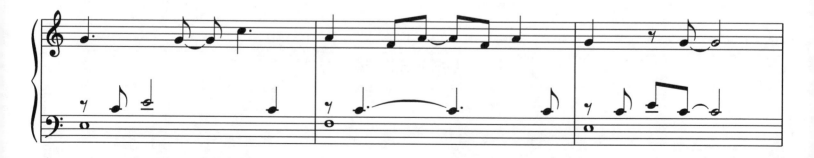

Repeat and Fade

Optional Ending

THE 7 METALS OF ALCHEMY

from FRESH AIRE 7

By CHIP DAVIS

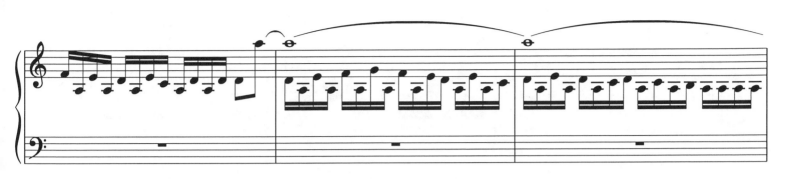

DANCIN' IN THE STARS
from FRESH AIRE V

By CHIP DAVIS

Repeat 3 times and Fade

WASSAIL, WASSAIL
from MANNHEIM STEAMROLLER CHRISTMAS

Arranged by CHIP DAVIS

THE FOURTH DOOR
from FRESH AIRE II

By CHIP DAVIS

SONATA BACH'S LUNCH
from DINNER

By CHIP DAVIS

Moderately, in a groove (♩ = 80)

To Coda ⊕

THE HOLLY & THE IVY
from A FRESH AIRE CHRISTMAS

Arranged by CHIP DAVIS

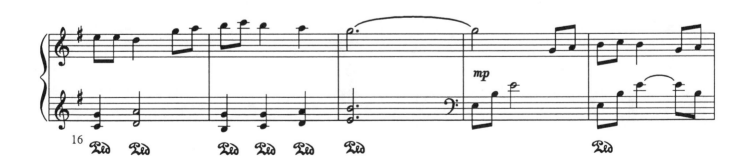

ECLECTIC BLUE
from PARTY 2

By CHIP DAVIS

HARP SEALS
from SAVING THE WILDLIFE

By CHIP DAVIS

KANBAI
from ROMANCE

By CHIP DAVIS

Last time To Coda ⊕

1., 3.

2.

mf

f

D.C. al Coda
(with repeat)

RUSLAN AND LUDMILLA
from TO RUSSIA WITH LOVE

By MIKHAIL IVANOVICH GLINKA